I0760026

HOW TO AVOID BEING EATEN BY SHARKS... AND OTHER ADVICE

How to Avoid Being Eaten By Sharks ... And Other Advice
Walker Books Australia Pty Ltd
Gadigal and Wangal Country
Locked Bag 22,
Newtown NSW 2042 Australia
www.walkerbooks.com.au

Walker Books Australia acknowledges the Traditional Owners of the country on which we work, the Gadigal and Wangal peoples of the Eora Nation, and recognizes their continuing connection to the land, waters, and culture. We pay our respect to their Elders past and present.

A catalogue record for this book is available from the National Library of Australia

ISBN: 978 1 7616 0061 6

The illustrations for this book were created digitally
Typeset in 11.5 pt Sweater School
Printed and bound in China

10 9 8 7 6 5 4 3 2 1

HOW TO AVOID BEING EATEN BY SHARKS... AND OTHER ADVICE

John Larkin

Illustrated by Chrissie Krebs

WALKER BOOKS

AND SUBSIDIARIES

LONDON • BOSTON • SYDNEY • AUCKLAND

CHAPTER 1

HOW TO AVOID BEING EATEN BY SHARKS

"The number of fatal shark attacks that have occurred in Liechtenstein is zero."

The Big Book of Interesting Facts – Volume 16

There is one absolute, sure-fire method to avoid being eaten by sharks. Don't go in the ocean. When you enter the ocean, you are in the shark's domain. If a shark plonked itself down next to you on your sofa and started eating your Twisties, then it would be in yours. My guess is that you wouldn't be entirely happy about that, particularly if it gobbled down the rest of your Twisties along with the family cat. So if you don't want this to happen, don't let them in your home. And don't go in theirs.

Okay, pretty obvious, but people don't always do the obvious thing. When authorities erect a sign that reads **NO FISHING FROM BRIDGE** it's pretty obvious that you shouldn't actually fish

from the bridge. But go there any night and you'll find about fifty people with their lines dangling in the water. Some of them will even lean their fishing rods against the sign or hang their catch from it.

If there's a large mud puddle in the middle of the school oval and the teachers say, "Woe betide anyone who goes near that puddle" (because teachers still use words like "woe betide"), you can bet that by the end of the day about 50 boys will have leaped into the puddle, drawn to it like spawning salmon.

Girls, on the whole, tend to avoid puddles, except for occasionally caking the mud onto their faces as they mature. They do this for largely unspecified reasons.

The fact remains that while there have been shark attacks in rivers and harbors, the majority of fatal encounters occur in the ocean. There has not, at the time of writing, been a recorded shark fatality of anyone who was, say, in a treehouse, playing Xbox in their bedroom, hanging out in a mall, riding a bike through the bush, playing cricket, eating Twisties on their sofa with the family cat etc, etc, or any other of the many non-ocean-based activities designed to prevent you from being devoured by sea creatures.

BEWARE OF THE ... STUFF

Let's be clear about this. The ocean is a dangerous place for biped, apelike creatures such as you. In fact, the ocean is so deadly that you'd swear it was out to get you. It isn't, of course. The ocean doesn't care – which sort of makes it worse, if you think about it. The ocean will kill you without even trying.

Aside from sharks, a list of things that are more than capable of killing you includes:

- RIPS

- ROGUE WAVES

- OIL TANKERS
- DROWNING
- DEHYDRATION
- SEA SNAKES

- BLUE-RINGED OCTOPUSES
- STONEFISH

- BREECHING WHALES
- STINGRAYS
- BOX JELLYFISH
- PUFFERFISH

- SALTWATER CROCODILES

- MORAY EELS
- NEEDLEFISH
- FLOWER URCHINS
- TEXTILE CONE SNAILS

- LIONFISH
- BARRACUDAS
- BOGANS ON BOOGIE BOARDS

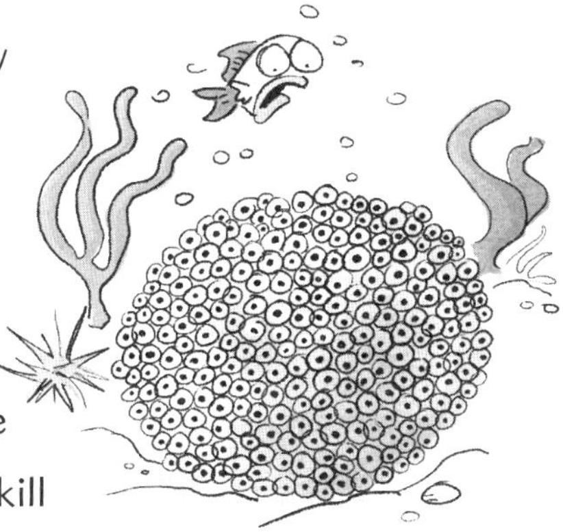

Given the above, why anyone ever sets foot in the ocean is a complete mystery. This is an environment so hostile to humans that even the flowers and snails can kill you. You clearly have a greater chance of survival leaping into a vat of acid wearing an inflatable pink unicorn around your waist than you do in the ocean.

Chances are, however, that at some point in your life, you're going to be called on to venture into the ocean whether you like it or not. We are, after all, a nation that is girt by sea. And people are always banging on about learning to swim and about surf education. The irony is that your surf educator will instruct you on how to avoid this, how to stay away from that – while there's a seething wall of watery death bearing down on you like Poseidon's fist. Teaching children surf education by dragging them into the ocean is a bit like educating you about the dangers of snakes by hurling you into a pit of writhing cobras.

But take sharks. They're not all deadly of course. Many are about as threatening as a basket of puppies and you could actually bring them home to play with your grandmother in your wading pool if either she or you wanted it. However, it's

probably advisable not to remove sharks from their ocean habitat for two reasons. First, it is illegal to cart sharks to and from the ocean for the express purpose of playing with your grandmother in your wading pool. Second, they will probably die (the shark, that is – not your grandmother). The back of your car, even if you own a spacious RV, is not a natural environment for marine life. Additionally, your wading pool will probably be heavily chlorinated due to the amount of peeing that takes place in it, and sharks generally have a reduced life expectancy when exposed to heavily chlorinated or urinated water.

BEWARE OF SOFAS

Before venturing any further, let's put things into perspective a little bit. The number of people killed worldwide by shark attacks in 2021 was nine. NINE. Conversely, according to the IFLScience website, the number of sharks killed by people during the same period was over 100 million. And that is a conservative estimate. Sharks, it appears, don't do too well in their encounters with humans. You, on the other hand, have a greater chance of being killed by a lightning strike, toppling vending machine, or plummeting sofa than you have of being "taken" by a shark. And that is if you are a regular ocean visitor. If you never set foot in the sea, you have a greater chance of being killed by a guinea pig, a Christmas decoration, or a steaming mound of horse dung.

And while we're on a roll, consider a few other things that are far more deadly than sharks. Your bed is a dangerous place. Approximately 450 people die each year from falling out of theirs. And the next time you feel the urge to take a selfie, you might want to rethink. More people die in this endeavor (usually from toppling backward over a cliff) than die from shark attacks worldwide. Flying champagne corks take out around 12 people annually, whereas plummeting coconuts account for over 10 times that number, and falling TVs take out a further 40. Messy handwriting kills around 7,000 people every year. Now before you scratch your head to a state of baldness, the messy handwriting generally belongs to a doctor who prescribes a drug or a dose that the pharmcist can't read.

As a left-hander, I'm bothered by the next one. Around 2,500 of my fellow lefties die each year from using a right-handed product incorrectly. That's it! I'm never leaving my bedroom again. Oh, wait a minute. My bed's in there and we've seen how dangerous beds are ... I'm lucky I've even made it through the paragraph at this rate.

This is all before we've even begun to discuss cows. It's hard to fathom but cows kill about 22 people each year in the US alone. I'm not sure what's happening in the rest of the world with regards to cow-induced fatalities as there are no records. Maybe the people who go around recording how many people are killed each year by cows, are killed by cows.

In a jaw-dropping subplot, a cow once fell from the sky and landed on a Japanese fishing trawler and sunk it. How did it get up in the sky in the first place? Well that's an udder story.

All that aside, if you insist on diving into the ocean, here are three shark species that might cause you a bit of a problem:

TIGER SHARKS

So called because they bear an uncanny resemblance to tigers. Though it's unlikely that you'll encounter one as you trek through the Indian jungle.

Actually, they look nothing like tigers, largely because they're fish. Because they are a bit stripy, they might just as well have been named after something else with stripes – "barcode sharks" or "toothpaste sharks", for instance. The name would certainly reduce the panic factor if one turned up at your favorite swimming spot or your grandmother's wading pool, "Quick, everyone out of the water! Toothpaste shark alert."

Tiger sharks tend to inhabit warm tropical waters, which means you're safe in Sydney or Melbourne, particularly if you are on George or Collins Street.

So unless *your* chosen habitat is the deep tropical ocean, or if you're reading this and happen to be a seal, squid or a turtle, or you end up castaway like Tom Hanks when he was stranded on that island in that castaway movie, "Bloke Stuck on an Island with a Volleyball" or something, then you are generally not going to be bothered by these guys.

BULL SHARKS

If tiger sharks look nothing like tigers, then whoever named bull sharks should not be allowed out in public unsupervized. A Himalayan yak looks more like a shepherd than a bull shark resembles the sneering, snorting quadruped that it's named after.

When I was a young boy fresh off the boat from England in the early '70s, our family lived for a time in Georges Hall in south-western Sydney, just next to Bankstown Airport. During an outing on the first full day in our adopted country, I was stunned to see a sign posted on the banks of the Georges River, less than a mile from our home (but almost 24 miles from the sea) that read **NO SWIMMING – SHARKS**. Due to my age and therefore limited grasp of the English language, I wasn't sure if the sign was telling the sharks not to swim there, or if it was warning people not to swim there because of them. A local myth claimed that a woman had attempted to leap into the river from nearby Milperra Bridge. It was said that she survived the fall (it's not that big a drop) but landed right in the jaws of a shark, which promptly chomped off both her arms, possibly in shock. Miraculously the woman survived and went on to live a happy life.

Even as a 6-year-old, I had a problem with this story. If the woman was upset before her encounter with the shark, how did she cope with the challenges that had placed her on the bridge in the first place – minus both arms? Thanks to the internet, it's easy now to debunk such urban myths, rather than having to rely on some 80-year-old eyewitness on the river bank with a stick and some sort of poodle-like thing.

The attack under Milperra Bridge took place on New Year's Eve 1934 next to Kentucky Reserve, about one mile north of the bridge. The woman was actually a girl of 13, Beryl Morrin. She wasn't the least bit upset and hadn't jumped from any bridge, but had in fact been swimming in the river at dusk with her mother and siblings. She did, however, lose both her arms in the attack, emerging from the churning and crimson water with a couple of bleeding shoulders and, you might imagine, a perplexed expression. Despite this, Ms Morrin went on to live a relatively normal and, by all accounts, happy and productive life, dying a local legend at the ripe old age of 92.

There had been other fatal shark attacks in the Georges River before her mauling, which begs the question why swimming wasn't prohibited – though there were safe areas cordoned off for swimmers. In 1903 William Price was taken by a shark after he and his friends' hired boat had capsized. Just three years later, 33-year-old William Dobson was fatally wounded by a shark near Lugarno. And just four hours prior to Morrin's encounter, Richard Soden was attacked and killed quite possibly by the same shark that would later severely wound young Beryl. Soden was attacked in the Vale of Ah, which is a little to the south of Milperra Bridge and so perhaps the two attacks have morphed into one, with the tale growing in the telling as the years went on.

Given the location, however, there can be little doubt as to the perpetrator of these fishy crimes – a bull shark.

The bull shark is unique in that it can make its way up brackish tributaries such as rivers and creeks and into the fresh water beyond. A group of them even took up residence in the landlocked lake of Brisbane's Carbrook Golf Club. A few juveniles are believed to have been swept into the lake during a flood in the early 1990s and due to the abundance of fish in the lake, the sharks had not only survived but thrived. If you happen to hit your brand-new Titleist Pro golf ball into this particular body of water then may I suggest you leave it, or else send your little brother in after it. And if your friends insist on invoking the you-must-play-the-ball-where-it-lies rule, then it's probably time to be on the lookout for new friends. The most predictable thing about bull sharks is their **UNPREDICTABILITY**.

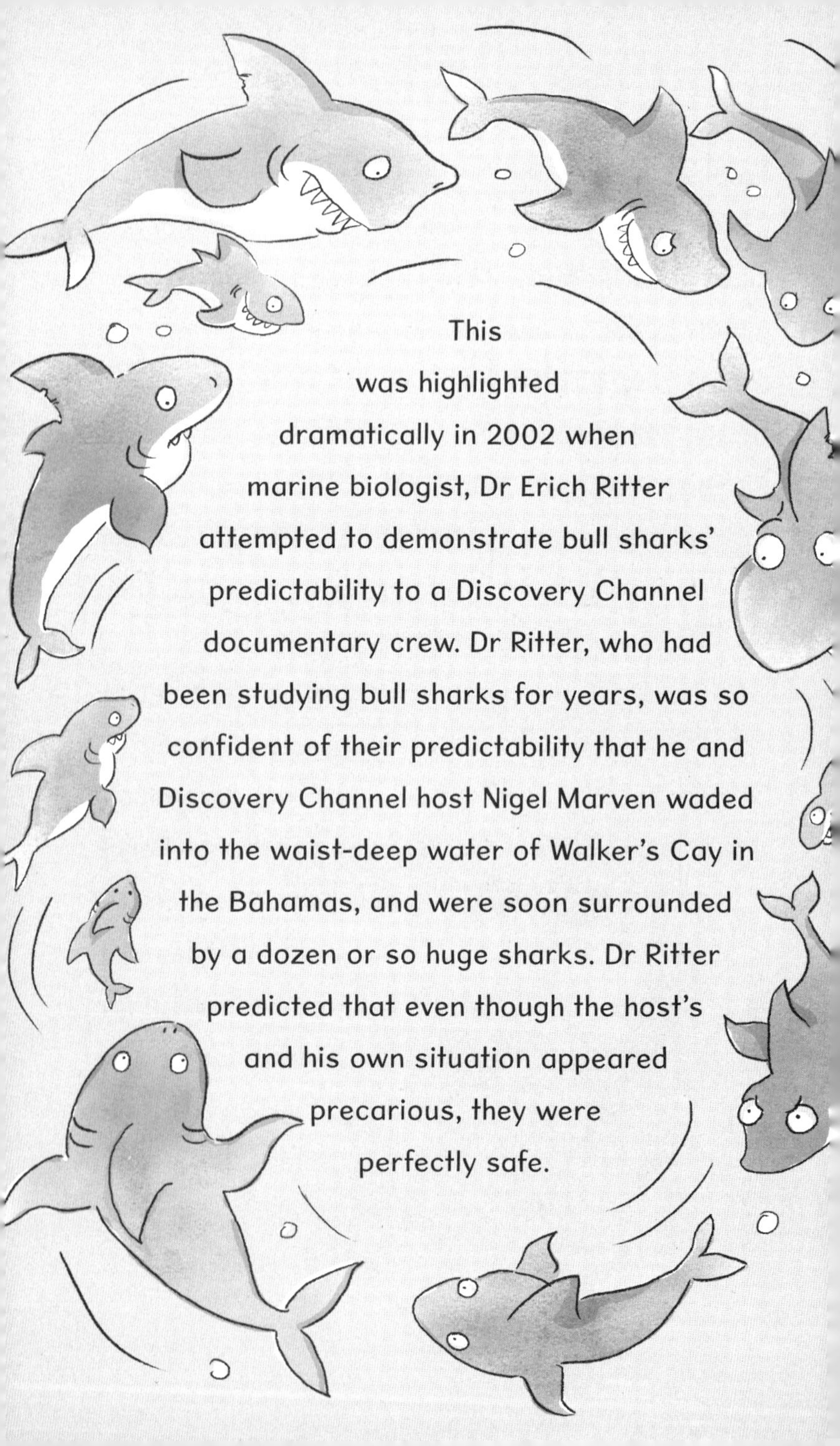

This was highlighted dramatically in 2002 when marine biologist, Dr Erich Ritter attempted to demonstrate bull sharks' predictability to a Discovery Channel documentary crew. Dr Ritter, who had been studying bull sharks for years, was so confident of their predictability that he and Discovery Channel host Nigel Marven waded into the waist-deep water of Walker's Cay in the Bahamas, and were soon surrounded by a dozen or so huge sharks. Dr Ritter predicted that even though the host's and his own situation appeared precarious, they were perfectly safe.

He knew these sharks and had waded in dozens of times with the same predictable outcome. His prediction held good right up to the moment one of the bull sharks, perhaps unaware of its own predictability, sidled up behind him and proceeded to remove a significant portion of his leg. Although Dr Ritter survived and surgeons saved what they could of his leg, he was essentially left with no calf muscle and now walks with a pronounced limp.

I'm trying to imagine how the conversation with the chief trauma surgeon went when Dr Ritter was wheeled into surgery:

SURGEON: This is one of the worst shark bites I've ever seen. Did you fall out of a boat?

DR RITTER: No. I stood in the water surrounded by about a dozen sharks and pretty much rang the dinner bell.

SURGEON: Nurse! Get the straitjacket and call security.

DR RITTER: I didn't predict *that*.

The year is 1916, a summer heatwave and thousands of holidaymakers flock to the Jersey Shore, the coastal region south of New York City. In 12 days 6 people are attacked by a shark or sharks and only one of them, 14-year-old Joseph Dunn, survives to tell the tale, though he is severely injured and almost loses a leg.

The first victim is the evocatively named Charles Epting Vansant, 23, who is swimming at Beach Haven late in the afternoon. Although he survives the initial attack, he dies from blood loss shortly afterward. A few days later along the same stretch of coastline, Charles Bruder, 27, is practically bitten in half by a shark. Although he is dragged into a rescue boat, there is significantly less of him than had entered the water, and he dies almost immediately.

The other attacks take place further up the coast in Matawan Creek. Believe it – **A CREEK**.

On July 12 Lester Stillwell, 11, is swimming with his friends in the creek when a dorsal fin breaks the surface and heads right for them. Realising that it's a shark, the group swims to the bank but Stillwell isn't fast enough. The shark drags him under and he meets a gruesome end. The surviving boys run to town and return with a rescue party including local tailor Watson Stanley Fisher, 23. Displaying incredible bravery – though he doesn't believe the boys when they tell him it's a shark – Fisher leaps into the water and manages to locate Stillwell's body. He is swimming back to the bank with Stillwell's remains when he too is fatally mauled.

Half an hour later, and less than a mile downstream from where Stillwell and Fisher were attacked, Joseph Dunn has his encounter with the shark but is rescued by his brother and friends, who engage in a tug-of-war with the shark for Dunn's life.

The Jersey Shore shark attacks are thought to be the inspiration behind Peter Benchley's seminal novel, *Jaws* and subsequent film by Steven Spielberg. In both the book and film the eponymous antagonist is identified as a great white shark. However, given that all three 1916 attacks occurred in the brackish tributary Matawan Creek, some 11 miles from the ocean, the culprit is more likely a bull shark. Or else there were two sharks – a great white patrolling the beaches and a bull shark in the creek. Or, given the high salinity levels in Matawan Creek, it could have been an old or juvenile great white shark. Whatever the truth, the evidence to convict either shark is inconclusive.

What is conclusive, however, is that outside the fictional world of *Jaws*, there has never been anything like the Jersey Shore attacks, before or since.

But this brings us to the third species you should look out for …

GREAT WHITE SHARKS

The Latin name for the great white shark is *charcharodon carcharias*, in English "Big Scary Meanie" – well, not quite, but it should be. *Charcharodon carcharias* actually translates as "sharp teeth". Which is kind of like, duh! Its Latin name should probably be something like *cisternina acuti morsu*, which sort of means "tank with teeth".

Prior to *Jaws*, pretty much all sharks rated equally on the scare-ometer. In fact, when my

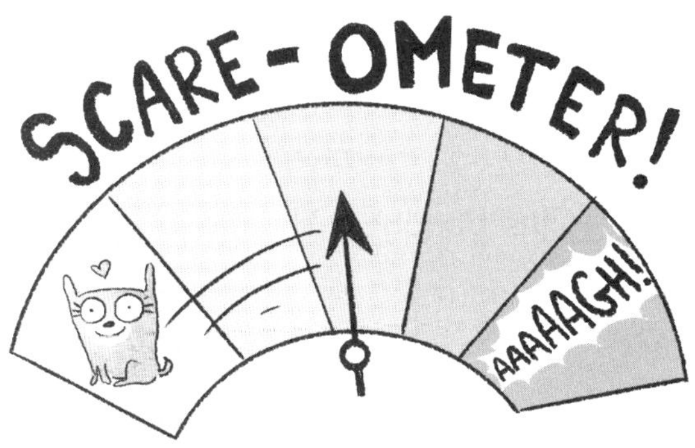

family arrived in Australia in 1970, we knew nothing of the great white shark or its river-lurking cousin, the bull shark. The one we were told to keep an eye on was the gray nurse shark. As it turns out the gray nurse is about as threatening as your average poodle. It's the kind of shark you could safely bring home to play with your grandmother in the wading pool. It's a popular attraction in aquariums, however, because it's large and appears quite fearsome with its protruding needle-like teeth. Little kids often hide behind Mom's legs when a gray nurse cruises by at the aquarium, because, well, little kids – brain size. You get the picture.

Jaws changed all that.

The story of *Jaws* centers on a rogue great white that acquires a taste for human flesh, stakes (or steaks) out its territory, and promptly goes on a homicidal rampage. This sends everyone in the fictional setting of Amity Island into a mass panic and ends up driving people from the water and tourists from the beaches. The movie had a similar effect, focusing as it did on people's primeval fear

of being eaten alive, and this had a huge impact on those economies that relied on beachside tourism.

The third act of *Jaws* involves an unlikely team setting out on a rusty old boat, which is essentially a weather-beaten shed with an engine attached, to slaughter the toothy leviathan. The trio consists of a junior marine biologist, Hooper (played by Richard Dreyfuss), the local police chief with an almost crippling case of aquaphobia, Brody (Roy Scheider), and salty old fisherman, who is quite clearly barking mad, Quint (Robert Shaw). Their near criminal incompetence is perhaps a metaphor for just how out of their depth humans are in the ocean, but just toward the end of the movie, Brody manages to pierce the oxygen tank that the shark is eating, with a bullet. The tank explodes and rains down bits of shark for several minutes. No one is really sure why *Jaws* tries to eat the oxygen tank – unless it's for dessert, since he's just recently devoured Quint as the main course.

Steven Spielberg didn't make *Jaws* because people are terrified of great white sharks.

People are terrified of great white sharks because Steven Spielberg made *Jaws*. A clear case of the tail wagging the dog. Following the success of *Jaws*, great white sharks became public enemy number 1 and were hunted down, almost onto the endangered list.

Great whites are now protected in Australia and many other countries such as the US and South Africa and have staged something of a comeback.

In the movie, great white sharks are portrayed as monstrous, indiscriminate killing machines. In one of the many sequels, *Jaws* 27 maybe, a close relative of the original shark eats a helicopter. That's when you know your scriptwriters have run out of ideas. What's next – a ferris wheel? A windmill? You can almost see where the idea for *Sharknado* came from. Almost.

Great whites are frightening to look at, their brains are tiny, and they could easily bite you in half. Yet despite the terror they engender in us, we are simply not on their menu. If we were, then we would be being picked off from the beach shallows in the hundreds every week by these ultimate apex predators. Great whites prefer soft and blubbery meals such as seals and sea lions. Humans are largely bony, contain little by way of meat, and are not particularly edible. Although we are sometimes mistaken for seals or sea lions, following an initial taste test the shark will realize its mistake and spit us out – unfortunately, sometimes the wound is fatal. It's rare that a great white will devour a human entirely and so the term "man eater" is wildly inappropriate and exaggerated – sharks aren't picky and will eat women too! You have a far greater chance of surviving an encounter with a great white shark than you do a hippopotamus – and they're vegan.

SURVIVAL OF THE DAFTEST

If you absolutely insist on wading into the ocean then the best methods to avoid being eaten by sharks are as follows:

1. Sharks, as you know, live in mortal fear of bells. So if you're swimming at your favorite beach and the shark bell starts dinging, then **GET OUT OF THE WATER**. A combination of your removing yourself from the menu and the terrifying sound of the dinging bell will send the shark torpedoing out to sea.

2. Swim next to someone who has an open wound. This might sound paradoxical given that sharks are attracted to blood, but sharks have a relatively poor grasp of paradoxes. What they do understand, however, is blood. Sharks are so sensitive to blood that they can detect a single droplet of dried blood on the hull of the Voyager 1 space probe, which is currently about 14 billion miles from Earth. They can't, actually, but it would be great if they could. The fact remains that sharks do have an amazing capacity to detect blood, perhaps the best of any animal on the planet. So, if you swim next to someone who has an open wound, chances are the shark will hone in on them rather than you.
3. Swim next to someone who has an underwater death ray. Okay; there's no such thing. Not yet anyway. When they are invented, however, try swimming next to someone who has one and you should be okay. Well, you'll be better off than someone who's not swimming next to

someone with an underwater death ray or an open wound and stuff.

4. Move to Liechtenstein. There has not, at the time of writing, been a fatal shark attack in Liechtenstein. Most shark attacks occur in countries with an abundance of coastline. In fact, the three nations that have recorded most fatal shark attacks – the United States, South Africa, and Australia – are either partly or entirely girt by sea. Whereas nations that are landlocked, such as Bolivia, Paraguay, Afghanistan, Botswana, Bhutan, Switzerland, Hungary, have a combined total of zero fatal shark encounters. That can't be a coincidence. Liechtenstein goes even further.

It is a landlocked country surrounded by other landlocked countries, namely Switzerland and Austria. It is also rather small, the airport runway is L-shaped, you need to take your passport just to pop down to the shops for a carton of milk, and the whole country was recently tiled, so it's quite difficult for a shark to actually fit, or at least arrive unannounced. None of that is true, of course – apart from the landlocked bit. That is true. I would, however, stake what's left of my reputation on your never being attacked by a shark should you move to Liechtenstein. Especially if you remember to pack a shark bell, underwater death ray, and a friend with an open wound.

CHAPTER 2

IS THE EARTH REALLY FLAT?

"The number of sharks that live on a flat Earth is currently zero."
The Big Book of Interesting Facts – Volume 16

As surprising as it may seem, the Earth hasn't always been round – okay, spherical for you three-dimensional pedants. Our earliest ancestors lived on a flat Earth because that was what their observations told them. They also lived at the center of the universe, again because their senses told them so.

Ugg the cave dweller would have stepped out of his cave for his early morning stretch or bathroom break and noticed how the Sun moved around the Earth. He would also have noticed, had it been a particularly long pee, that later on the Moon would make a similar journey. Okay, the Moon changed

Waxing Gibbous

First Quarter

Full Moon

Waxing Crescent

Waning Crescent

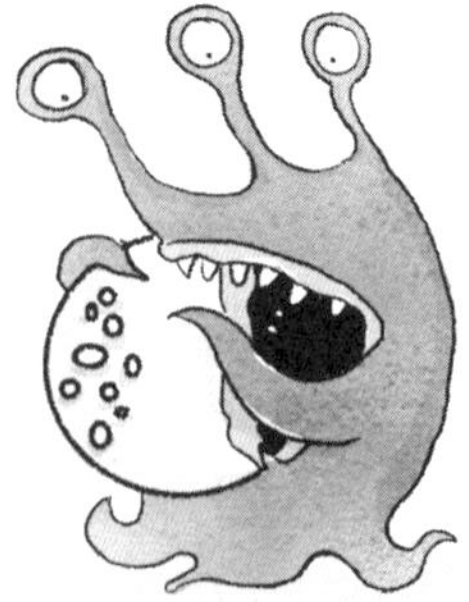

Third Quarter

Waning Gibbous

shape as the days passed, possibly having been bitten by some sort of invisible sky monster, but eventually a new Moon would replace the one that had been devoured and things would return to normal.

Ugg the cave dweller had no reason to think that the Earth was anything other than flat because that's how it was, no matter where he looked. Okay, there were some sticky up bits, which his descendants would eventually get around to calling mountains, but they were just anomalies as far as Ugg was concerned. Also, Moon-eating monsters probably lived on the other side of the sticky up bits, so it was best not to bother going into or beyond them. Had Ugg the cave dweller been particularly adventurous, he could have set off walking (oceans notwithstanding) and after a particularly energetic trek of some 25,000 miles, he would have arrived right back at his cave, which would probably have confused the heck out of him.

Funnily enough, despite not knowing that the Earth was round, Ugg the cave dweller would have understood gravity to some degree, though not necessarily what it was called or what to do about it. He would have accepted, for instance, that if a mammoth chased him over a cliff, it would hurt like hell when he got to the bottom, especially if the mammoth was still behind him. Actually, Ugg knew more science than he probably let on. At some level, he knew that despite their different weights, he and the mammoth would fall at the same rate. In essence, Ugg the cave dweller understood Newton's Second Law of Motion *(Fnet = ma)* hundreds of thousands of years before Newton and his apple cropped up.

As surprising as it may seem, and although he probably couldn't put it into words, largely because he didn't know any, Ugg understood that "The acceleration of an object as produced by a net force is directly proportional to the magnitude of the net force, in the same direction as the net force, and inversely proportional to the mass of the object." That really is mind-blowing until you realize that my cats know exactly the same thing.

E = MEOW C^2

At my house we have a tall back fence which the cats enjoy sitting on so they can be admired by passers-by and make faces at the local dogs out for an afternoon stroll. When they want to come inside for food, or because there are no passers-by to admire them or dogs to poke fun at, they know that if they jump from the top of the fence they will accelerate more before they collide with the mass that is exerting the force (the Earth).

So in order to decrease their acceleration time, they will crawl headfirst down the fence until they get as low as they can, and only then will they jump. Incidentally, in order for my cats to reach terminal velocity (the maximum speed that can be obtained during freefall), it would take around 12 seconds with their limbs spreadeagled. However, in order for them to actually reach terminal velocity, my back fence would need to be about 280 miles high, which would certainly reduce the number of tennis balls that come hurtling over from the neighbor's court.

DOWN UNDER

But enough of physics-aware ancient cave dwellers and contemporary cats. Let's get back to the shape of the Earth.

As a child, I too thought the Earth was flat because nobody bothered to tell me otherwise. When I was 5 years old, my parents announced that we were moving to Australia. I didn't know where Australia was or how we would go about getting there. My mother who, like a lot of people from Yorkshire,

was big on adjectives and tautology, told me that we would be sailing there on a great, big, massive ship. When I shared my momentous news at school, one of my friends informed me that Australia was down under. From this I deduced that at some point on the voyage we would plummet over a sort of huge waterfall on our great, big, massive ship and then sail under the Earth until we arrived in Australia, which, according to my school sage, was upside down. Apparently everyone in Australia was fitted with spiked shoes that stuck in the ground to prevent them falling off the Earth. This prepubescent intellectual, whose name I've forgotten largely because he was barking mad, also had it on good authority that snakes roamed the streets and strange men in corked hats rode wallabies down to the beach and beat off spiders the size of dinner plates with their didgeridoos

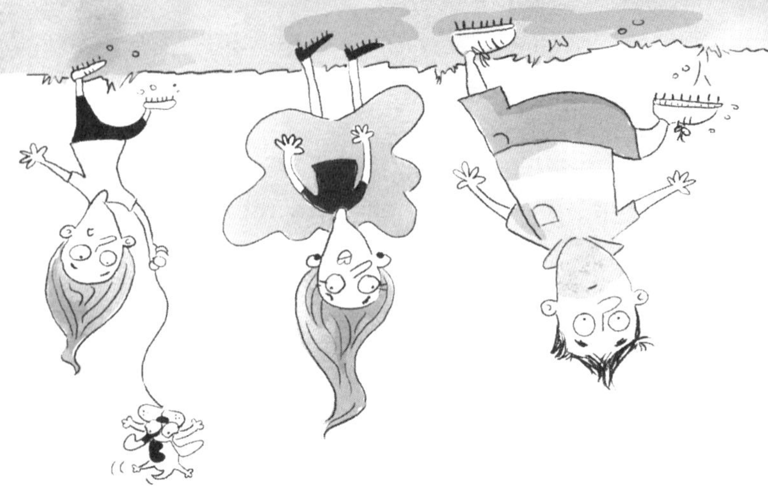

and boomerangs. I wondered if the wallabies were also adorned with spiked shoes or whether they got around with some sort of organic suction pads on the soles of their feet. Please remember that I was 5 years old – brain size, remember? You get the picture.

But let's leave the younger me and my moment of insanity for a moment and return to how the world was transformed from flat to round.

TWINKLE TWINKLE, LITTLE STAR

It all started about 2,000 years ago. The ancient Greeks were enlightened scientists, mathematicians and philosophers who dramatically changed the way we viewed the world. One of them, Socrates, was so radical in his thinking that he was arrested and put on trial, basically for being a bit of a know-it-all. Found guilty of extreme smart aleckry, he was sentenced to death and forced to drink hemlock, which is not really something you want packed in your school lunch. It was Socrates's contemporary, Aristotle, who pointed out that the Earth was round when he observed that there was a different set of stars and constellations visible depending on where you were, which simply wouldn't be the case if the Earth was flat. A little later, another Greek philosopher and mathematician, Eratosthenes,

actually managed to measure the circumference of the Earth. He set off walking with an incredibly long tape measure and didn't stop until—

No, he didn't actually. Instead he measured the distance between two cities and the angle of the Sun's relative position overhead at noon, and used trigonometry to calculate the circumference of the Earth to a surprising degree of accuracy.

Polish-born Nicolaus Copernicus (1473–1543) further expounded the round Earth view by introducing the paradigm-shifting idea of a heliocentric (Sun-centered) universe. Copernicus's theories were resolutely rejected by the all-powerful Catholic Church as they removed "man" from the center of the universe where God had placed "him". There certainly was, and always has been, a surplus of testosterone surging through the veins of the decision-makers, and perhaps we're starting to zero in on the problem. Eventually, though, Copernicus was excommunicated for his troubles, which was kind of like being made to sit in the naughty corner and write a reflection.

And that was the thing. You didn't want to upset the status quo too much with your revolutionary ideas. Consider the plight of Giordano Bruno (1548–1600), whose theories were even more radical than Copernicus's. Giordano Bruno was a philosopher, friar (religious, not the chip and scallop/potato cake sort), mathematician, poet, and cosmological theorist. The unfortunate polymath went further than Copernicus by having the audacity to propose that the stars were distant suns, just like ours, quite possibly with planets of their own, and what was more, these planets might contain life. He even went as far as suggesting that the universe had no center and was in fact infinite. This too went against the prevailing wisdom of the Church and the Earth-centered finite universe that God had created. Well Pope Clement VIII wasn't having any of that nonsense because if he, as God's representative on Earth, was wrong, that meant God was wrong too. And while God may have been many things, ignorant wasn't one of them.

The unfortunate Giordano Bruno was summoned to appear before the Inquisition, who were basically a bunch of self-righteous zealots (somewhere between priests and storm troopers) who you really didn't want to get on the wrong side of. Friar Bruno was found guilty of heresy and sentenced to death. On the day of his execution, the unfortunate visionary had his tongue imprisoned, which is even nastier than it sounds, was hung upside down and finally burned at the stake and his ashes were unceremoniously dumped into the

River Tiber. You can almost imagine Pope Clement VIII walking away from the river, wiping his ash-covered hands on his papal robes with a, “So there.”

'RELEASE THE KRAKEN!'

Despite the plight of the ill-fated Giordano Bruno, eventually we were able to assimilate the concept of a spherical Earth into our way of thinking.

Previously, when we took to the seas, the greatest peril that sailors faced, apart from sea monsters, krakens, and gigantic whirlpools, was to sail off the edge of the Earth and plummet into the void of space.

The matter was finally settled when the Portuguese explorer, Ferdinand Magellan, circumnavigated the world between 1519 to 1522 without once encountering any sort of edge or kraken.

And that was the end of the issue. Or so we thought.

Recently there has been a renaissance in flat-Earth thinking (though "thinking" might be overstating it). The so-called evidence presented by the flat-Earth cult is so easily countered that even our friend Ugg the cave dweller would have laughed it off, had he not been silenced by falling mammoths. My interest in science and particularly physics does not make me a scientist or a physicist, but if you really want to see flat-Earthers and their questionable theories destroyed by a real scientist, pop over to YouTube and check out "Professor Dave Explains". What fascinates me is why people, despite the overwhelming evidence to the contrary, need to believe that the Earth is flat.

First of all, flat-Earthers have no trouble accepting that the Sun, the Moon, the planets of our solar system, and pretty much every other celestial body are all spherical. And therein lies the rub, methinks. As previously discussed, prior to the Greek philosophers and other deep thinkers and scientists such as Copernicus, Galileo, and the unfortunate Giordano Bruno, the Earth was not only flat, it was the center of the universe. Being the center of the universe was pretty important and those pesky scientists took it away from us and we ended up an irrelevant blue dot in a minor solar system. A solar system that doesn't even have a name: it's just called "the solar system", like if you went to a school that was called "the school", or played cricket for a team that was just called "the team". It's not even worth a proper noun. We now know that our galaxy is fairly ordinary and one of billions of galaxies, but even it has a real name: The Milky Way – though whoever decided to call it after a chocolate bar should be taken outside and given a good talking-to.

Speaking of names, William Herschel is another one who should be up for a bit of a scolding. For those unfamiliar with his areas of expertize, Herschel was the astronomer/composer who discovered and named Uranus, presumably after a severe bout of food poisoning when his wife walked into the bathroom, saw that her husband was still perched on the toilet and said, "William, would you like some ointment for—" You can guess the rest.

Perhaps, like the succession of popes who denied the evidence of a heliocentric solar system because it meant they were no longer the center of the universe, flat-Earthers also need to be at the center of things. A flat Earth, with all the other spherical heavenly bodies orbiting around us, relocates us back to the center of the universe. This takes us from a heliocentric solar system to an egocentric universe. We then move from being a tiny, insignificant blue speck floating in infinite

we are here!

nothingness, to the nucleus of everything there is, has been, or ever will be. It turns out that our flat-Earthers aren't just ignorant, they're narcissistic as well.

WE LIVE ON AN EMU'S BUTT

Despite the overwhelming evidence to the contrary, flat-Earthers remain resolute in their stubbornness, claiming that the evidence supporting a round Earth is a hoax and that the rest of us are in on a great conspiracy to deny their truth.

The simplest way to respond to a flat-Earther is not to show them the reams of scientific, pictorial, and video evidence, because they will just dismiss it. For a non-scientist such as me, it comes down to two bits of irrefutable logic.

First, if it is a conspiracy by us round-Earthers to keep the truth about the shape of our planet a secret, then it is rather pointless. You, me, and everyone else who knows and accepts that the Earth is round, gain absolutely nothing from the Earth actually being round. Nothing. Zip. Niente. If the overwhelming empirical evidence presented by actual scientists, rather than someone with an opinion and an IP address living in his mother's basement, showed that the Earth was flat, cylindrical, triangular or banana-shaped, then we would accept it. I for one am not shape-ist.

I don't need the Earth to be round in order to function. I would carry on as normal even if the Earth turned out to be the shape of an emu's butt. Okay, I probably would be a tad embarrassed if aliens turned up and I actually lived on a planet that was the shape of an overgrown starling's posterior.

But that would be my problem, not the aliens'.

Second, while much that is negative can be laid at the feet of humanity, it is also fair to say that we are quite an adventurous species. If the Earth is flat, then it's a reasonable proposition that someone with an enterprising spirit and deep pockets – some billionaire tycoon or other – might have put together an expedition to check out the edge of the Earth and take a couple of selfies for his social media platforms. Or that some other person of means might have seen a dollar or two in building a platform out over the edge and offering customers the chance to bungy jump into the void. I'd certainly want a go.

Getting into a debate with a flat-Earther is a bit like playing chess with a chicken. The chicken knows it's got zero chance, but it will peck away at you regardless. It's not the same as having an argument or discussion over who is the better footballer, Messi or Ronaldo. Both

sets of fans could claim that their guy is the GOAT (greatest of all time), as could Pele's, Maradona's, Zidane's or the original Brazilian Ronaldo's. Who is the greatest player of all time? It's not based on objective facts. It's a subjective opinion. Personal preference. The shape of the world isn't an opinion. It's a fact.

Serious scientists, such as world-renowned astrophysicist Neil deGrasse Tyson, don't even bother discussing flat-Earth theories, because

to do so would give such insanity a modicum of respectability. And to try and educate someone whose mind is so closed to the truth, would be a bit like trying to explain Einstein's Theory of Relativity to a yogurt.

Sometimes the simplest response is the best. I'll leave the final word on the subject to Bill Nye the Science Guy. "Is the Earth flat or round? It's round."

Enough said.

CHAPTER 3

HOW TO TRANSLATE PARENT-SPEAK

"If you're pulling a face and the wind changes, your face will NOT stay that way."
The Big Book of Interesting Facts – Volume 16

Once, following some sort of childhood transgression, my mother, through gritted teeth, informed me that she was going to give me a "good hiding" that would take me to "within an inch of my life". As so much time has passed since that day, I can't recall exactly what I had done to warrant such harsh punishment. It might have had something to do with my inviting a mangy wet stray dog to sleep in her bed while it recovered from a bad case of diarrhoea. As I didn't particularly relish the idea of being taken to a place that was within an inch of my life, I tore off toward the horizon with my arms flailing. Upon reaching the safety of the horizon, where there was a disused cowshed I could hide in, it suddenly dawned on me what a strange threat this was. She was going to take me to within an inch of my life? Surely proximity to death would be measured in units of time, not distance.

When I sheepishly returned home from the cowshed later that afternoon, my mother – rather than set about me with the cricket bat, branch or nunchucks – simply glared and said that she'd better not catch me doing anything like that again. Another strange expression, because she seemed to be saying that it was okay to do it again, as long as she didn't catch me.

My mother wasn't prone to fits of unfathomable rage or threats of violence, though as the daughter of a hard-as-nails Irish coalminer, she wasn't to be messed with either. Earlier that year I'd watched her confront half a dozen juvenile matchstick-flicking reprobates on a train. When a lit match landed in my sister's hair, my mother erupted. While the businessmen cowered behind their broadsheet newspapers, my mother beat out the flames on my sister's head, grabbed the loudest troublemaker and asked whether he wanted her to knock him into the middle of next week. I didn't realize what this particular threat entailed until much later – she was going to hit him so hard that he was going to end up in a week-long coma. I was impressed.

Clearly my mother knew exactly how much force was required to render someone unconscious for a seven-day period. The young man obviously didn't relish the thought of being hospitalized at the hands of a middle-aged woman, so the lot of them quietened down. They sprang to life again when we alighted at our station, the door was shut and the train began to depart. Only then did they feel confident enough to launch insults at my mother and break out the matches once more.

THE IMPORTANCE OF DUCKING

Despite her usual gentle nature, my mother had once hurled my younger brother's toy RPG (rocket-propeled grenade launcher) at my teenaged sister with the force of an actual RPG. Fortunately for both of them, what my mother made up for with power, she lacked in accuracy. My sister managed to duck as the missile hurtled by harmlessly over her head and smashed into the wall with such momentum that it left an RPG-shaped impression. It remained that way for some time until my father eventually patched it up shortly after he'd retired and they had put the house up for sale. As my sister went flailing from the house, screeching like a banshee whose skirt was on fire, my mother called after her, "Let that be a lesson to you!" I scratched my head and wondered just what sort of lesson had taken place.

Something along the lines of how to avoid having a toy rocket hurled at your head, I imagined. But it was a stretch.

Over the following weeks two further incidents made me question my mother's linguistic choices, if not her outright sanity. First, although it was getting dark, it was also the school holidays; so, after dinner, I asked her if I could go out and ride my skateboard for a bit. Already piqued about something that had happened earlier, she just gave me that look of hers and said, "I'll skateboard you, my laddo." No one had ever skateboarded me before, so I didn't know what to make or do with such a threat. I did wonder briefly if her skateboarding me involved attaching a set of wheels to various body parts and perhaps refashioning my torso out of wood. The following week it had been pouring with rain for a several days so my brother and I set about constructing a Lego mansion. Having run out of bricks before starting work on the eighth storey, I asked my mother if she could buy us some more Lego on the way home from work the next day. Once again I was on the sharp end of that glare, followed by a terse, "I'll give you Lego, my laddo!" We were confused. Her words suggested that we would actually *get* the Lego, but her tone indicated otherwise.

THE BARD OF BANKSTOWN

This way of speaking wasn't unique. The suburb we lived in was full of English migrant families, just like ours. Perhaps English people believed that, having invented the language, they could pretty much do as they liked with it. After all, isn't that what Shakespeare did? If he couldn't think of a word to fit the moment, he simply made one up.

But my mother wasn't an Elizabethan playwright from Stratford-upon-Avon; she was a pastry cook from Yorkshire, lived in Toongabbie, and worked in a cake shop in Bankstown. All our neighbours butchered the language with these confusing euphemisms too. My close friend's mother, who was also English, regularly threatened to box his ears for him, presumably because he couldn't box them himself. I was never able to hear this threat without picturing her assembling a couple of small wooden boxes around his ears. I only realized later that she was probably talking about the sport of boxing, and she was offering to step into a boxing ring with him to beat up his ears. Even as I write this, I'm not absolutely sure that's correct and I still imagine those wooden boxes around his ears.

As the years passed, I collected more of my mother's threats, some of which pushed the boundaries of logic to breaking point. On occasion, when my siblings and I descended into school holiday anarchy, my mother would abandon any attempt at parental control and hiss, "Just wait until your father gets home!" This didn't exactly strike the fear of God into us. Our father was an even-tempered Irishman (if there is such a thing) who was slow to anger and believed that matters of discipline rested firmly on shoulders other than his. Hearing of our misdemeanors, he'd shake his head and make a sort of "tuttsch, tuttsch, tuttsch"

noise, like a dog eating peanut butter. Then he would go out the back and mow the lawn, whether it needed mowing or not, mumbling about how he worked harder than a one-armed violinist.

As a young boy I had an aversion to steak. I found it inedible and would have rather eaten my own shoe, or someone else's. I didn't realize until later in life that this wasn't so much a reflection on my tastebuds, more my parents' culinary skills. Although my mother prides herself on being a good cook, she could not cook steak. The concept of marinade was alien to her and she clearly sourced the meat from some part of the cow that nobody had ever heard of. If in fact it was from a cow at all. My father wasn't a whole lot of help either.

Now unlike my mother, my father couldn't cook. He would fire up the BBQ until it reached thermonuclear meltdown level. He would then throw

on the meat and casually cremate it for about five hours or until every last ounce of moisture had evaporated. The charred result was similar to if, say, a possum decided to dive headfirst into a neutron star. Dear old Dad would deliver this repast to the table, wearing a hazmat suit and asbestos gloves. I would sit there staring at the grizzled lump of flesh wondering how I was going to make any headway. You didn't need a knife to eat steak at our house, more a scalpel.

Eventually I got wise and started turning

up at the dinner table wearing my thickest soccer socks. Now and then I'd smuggle chunks of chewed cow into my socks along with the broccoli, peas, and corn, and brussels sprouts (which should have been illegal anyway). At the end of the "meal" I would sneak out the back and feed the contents of my socks to the dog. By the end of the year I was bordering on malnourished, while the dog had to sign up for Weight Watchers as she started to resemble a beach ball with a couple of stubby legs sticking out the bottom.

But all that was in the future. My siblings quickly finished their dinner, though to this day I have no idea how. Perhaps they had their own techniques for smuggling their steak out to the dog, which would certainly explain why it looked like a walrus in a flea collar. And because siblings are essentially demon spawn, they would hide around the corner with the sole intention of making me laugh. They would pull faces and feign strangulation or death, knowing that if I were to burst out laughing I would be in serious trouble. However, the harder you try to suppress laughter, the more likely it will erupt out of your mouth, nose, or some other opening. It's like when you stare out the classroom window during an important test and you notice a bird with only one wing, perched on the ledge. The bird takes off, does a complete circle, and lands back in the exact same spot with a confused expression on its face. And *you're* the only one who's seen it. You spend the lesson trying to suppress the laughter as your head appears desperate to explode.

Despite my efforts, eventually a snort would erupt out of me, sort of like a pig in a pepperbush. My mother would march over to the table like she meant business and hiss, "You'll be laughing on the other side of your face in a minute." Laughing on the other side of my face? Surely the only way you could actually laugh on the other side of your face would be to undergo corrective surgery.

HOLY CAT

One of my fondest childhood memories was the result of a trip to our local church when I was about 11. The Church is quite big on forgiveness, which is kind of ironic given that it has much to be sorry for. Catholic confession back then worked like this. You entered a booth about the size of an old phone box. Meanwhile the priest sat in a connecting booth. You would tell him all the sins you had committed since you were last dragged to confession by your parents. The priest would absolve you of your sins but give you a penance, which meant you had to recite a whole bunch of Our Fathers and Hail Marys.

As a fairly squeaky-clean kid I used to have to make up sins so the priest would have something to forgive me for. And given the number of times we were dragged to confession (goodness knows what my parents were up to) I was forced to make up a long list.

And with the number of things I'd told him that I'd stolen over the years, the priest probably locked away the good cutlery whenever he saw us pull into the parking lot.

Then one brilliant day, something happened that temporarily broke us. My siblings and I were kneeling in a pew toward the center of the church contemplating our non-existent sins, while our parents were kneeling in the pew directly in front of us undergoing their hefty penance. I wondered for a moment if they had robbed a bank or something, because it sounded like they were working their way through a combined total of 4,000 Hail Marys.

Suddenly, without warning, a mangy old alley cat wandered into the church. From where we were, all we could see was a disembodied tail, meandering from pew to pew in search of redemption or mice. When neither was forthcoming, it made its way to the front of the church and jumped up onto the altar, where it began to drink the holy water. Depending on the strength of that Godly brew, the cat probably scored about 9,000 extra lives.

This was in 1974 but, given the amount of holy water it slurped down, that cat may still be alive and is possibly immortal. I imagined it being run over by a steamroller, standing up, brushing itself down, and stomping over to kick the massive steel roller.

The cat's sculling of the holy water was all too much. The three of us erupted. My sister, Trish, slipped sideways onto the pew and began beating it with her fists. My brother, Paul, slid off the pew like a snake and writhed around on the floor convulsing with laughter. I tried desperately to

hold it together as I could hear my mother's teeth grinding, but it was impossible. I covered my mouth in a futile attempt to suppress the laughter, but it burst out of my eyes and ears instead. My mother turned around and said one of the strangest things I've ever heard. "You'll be laughing in a minute!" This made it even worse and we laughed so hard that we may have even died that day from internal haemorrhaging and this is actually the afterlife.

But perhaps the oddest example of parent-speak I've ever heard was directed at my brother. No stranger to pushing the boundaries separating

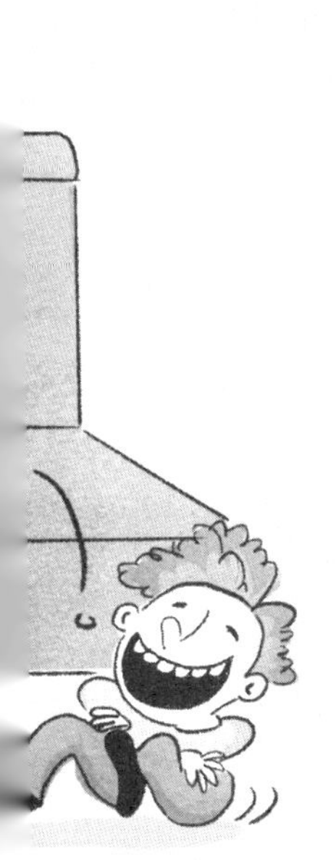

life from death, he and his best mate, Phil Beckett, once blew up the local electricity substation with a large metal spike, largely to see if it could be done. Once I had watched him ride his bike past a group of chatting mothers, including my own. Rather than cycle by in what one might call the "traditional" way, our young stunt rider was standing on the seat with one foot, and steering with the other. He was also probably doing something improbable, like riding with his eyes closed while juggling a Rubik's cube, a bowling ball, and a chainsaw. My mother took one look at this death-defying feat and said, "Don't come running to me when you're in a wheelchair!"

Not having heard these expressions for decades, I figured that time had deleted them from our language. However, on a recent trip to a shopping precinct near my home, I heard a young mother issue one of these threats to her crying child and I actually snorted when I heard it. The boy was clearly upset over being denied an ice-cream or permission to build an atomic bomb in the family shed. He was wailing like a goat in a gale. His mother, clearly embarrassed at the attention he was attracting, marched up to him and said, "I'll give you something to cry about!"

I'll leave the last word on this subject to my own mother. Recently I phoned her to wish her a happy birthday. Given her advanced years, I asked whether she had a fire extinguisher on standby in order to douse the flames that would surely spread out of control should she manage to light all the candles. There was a slight pause on the other end of the line while she considered her response. In the end she simply said,

"I'll fire-extinguish YOU, my laddo!"

PENICILLIN
INK

CHAPTER 4

HOW TO PASS YOUR CREATIVE WRITING TEST

The oldest known piece of writing was discovered in a cave in North Africa in 1963 and is believed to be around 10,000 years old. Translated it reads, "Darling. Before you come to bed, please don't forget to put the cat out."

The Big Book of Interesting Facts – Volume 16

You might be interested to know that the most important invention in the history of humanity isn't the computer, penicillin, the wheel, engine, pants, phone, the snout snuggy, or the fish training kit. No. The most important invention in history is writing.

Writing doesn't just entertain, it instructs, as it allows for the sharing of information and has done for eons before the internet turned up.

Have you ever played the game Whispers? A sentence or phrase is passed from one person to the next verbally by whispering (preferably without slobbering) in their ear. No matter how simple the sentence, by the time it's passed through the entire class it often bears little or no resemblance to how it started out. I once played this game with an advanced senior English class and the sentence, "A nod's as good as a wink to a blind horse", ended up,

"Donald Trump links to geese". However, when you write the original sentence down and pass it around the room, it comes out at the other end exactly as it was written, and Donald Trump doesn't get a look in, which is all kinds of right.

Could you imagine what might have happened to various inventions without writing?

The Manhattan Project was established by the US government in order to create the world's first nuclear weapon. The civilian head of the project was Dr Robert Oppenheimer, a theoretical physicist and all-round clever clogs, who would later regret his involvement in the project and call for nuclear weapons to be banned. After the first successful test detonation at Los Alamos, New Mexico in July 1945, Oppenheimer, upon realising what he and his team had done, and the potential for destruction that they had unleashed on the planet, was quoted as saying, "Now I am become Death, the destroyer of worlds." Actually he didn't say that. What he said was, *"kālo 'smi lokakṣayakṛt pravṛddho lokān samāhartum iha pravṛttaḥ"* which was a quote from the Bhagavad Gita, an ancient Hindu religious text, which translates into English as, "Now I am become Death, the destroyer of worlds".

Building a nuclear weapon now isn't as difficult as it once was, simply because it's been done before and there are written instructions on how to do it. Had the various steps not been written down and instead shared verbally (as in the Whispers game) we might not have ended up with a nuclear weapon but with shoe umbrellas, which, on reflection, might have been a good thing.

MY KINGDOM FOR A COMMA

The following is *not* a true story. Or is it?

When police burst into the Wilton family home in northern Sydney, they were surprized to find the entire family involved in an energetic and fun game of Scrabble.

They were further shocked to discover the Wiltons' pet dog, Patches, and cat, Buttons, asleep on a rug and cuddled up in each other's paws. In all respects, the Wilton family was a picture of domestic bliss and harmony, which wasn't what the police were expecting at all. What they imagined they would encounter, when they bulldozed their way through the Wiltons' wooden front door with their battering-ram thing, was some sort of cannibalistic, animal-sacrificing, and devouring ritual being perpetrated by the Wiltons' 11-year-old son, Adam.

Rather than tucking into a plateful of his parents, his little sister Sonia, along with Patches and Buttons and some hotdog rolls with BBQ sauce, Adam had spent the last half an hour trying to get rid of his troublesome Q tile without having a U to help him.

He looked up at the dozen or so tasers that were pointed directly at him and did what most 11-year-olds would do with even one taser pointed at them – he peed himself. The steaming yellow

liquid dribbled down his leg, taking with it his self-esteem. Or at least that's what he would write in his recount of the incident when he returned to school the following Monday. The sentence received a tick and a ☺ from his teacher, Ms Watt. She even awarded Adam one million house points (when her usual maximum was 10) for his writing. Adam figured that Ms Watt still felt guilty about the whole police-raiding-his-house-and-pointing-their-tasers-at-him-and-peeing-his-pants deal, but he didn't mind. The bonus one million house points saw Adam's house, Fitzwilliam, move to the top of the house points leader board, where it would remain for the rest of the year. Because Adam was a reasonable boy, he understood that the police incident wasn't all Ms Watt's fault and that he was at least partly responsible. The lesson that Adam took from having 12 police tasers pointed at him, and then peeing down his leg, was about the importance of punctuation.

No one, in the history of history, has ever been shot (or tasered) over punctuation before. I just checked. Adam, however, came closer than anyone else.

LET'S EAT GRANDMA

In order to fully understand how a couple of missing commas nearly led to Adam being pumped full of police-issue electricity, we need to go a couple of days back in time.

It was the first day of the school year and Adam's new teacher, Ms Watt, had devised a questionnaire in order to get to know her students. One of the questions asked for three things that the students were most passionate about.

Adam had filled out this questionnaire with his tongue poking out the side of his mouth, because it gave his brain more room to operate. When he came to the three things he was most passionate about, he simply included his family along with his dog and cat. Because he was also a keen chef, with his mongolian beef being the stuff of family legend, he'd also added this to the list. Unfortunately for Adam, when he wrote down his three things on Ms Watt's questionnaire, he'd neglected to use punctuation, believing it to be unimportant. So what he wrote was:

List 3 things you are passionate about:

I LOVE COOKING MY FAMILY AND PETS.

When Ms Watt began looking through the questionnaires at home on Saturday evening, with a large glass of fermented grape juice on hand, she'd taken one look at Adam's response and her eyes had widened to the size of a startled pufferfish. Fifteen minutes later, the SWAT team were breaking down the Wiltons' front door with tasers drawn.

As Adam found out, punctuation is important and can help prevent you from, among other things, being zapped by a dozen police tasers, or inadvertently eating your grandmother.

What? Eating grandmothers? Well, if you still doubt the importance and life-sustaining qualities of punctuation, consider this. In the following sentence you are taking your grandmother into a restaurant: *Let's eat, Grandma.* If, however, you forget the comma, your grandmother moves from dinner guest to main course: *Let's eat Grandma.*

The English language can be a strange and unwieldly beast. Consider the fabled nonsense word *ghoti* that English teachers often roll out on the first day of the school year, primarily to show their students just how clever they are. Most people would probably pronounce it "goat" with "ee" on the end. As it happens, the English language can turn *ghoti* into, wait for it, *fish.*

Now before you start scratching your head so hard that you're in danger of hitting brain, let's see how this is possible.

First you take the *gh* of a word such as *rough*. Unlike the *gh* in ghost, the gh in rough makes an *f* sound.

Next you take the *o* from the plural of *woman*, which is *women.* The *o* here makes neither a long nor a short *o* sound, but rather a short *i.*

Finally you take the *ti* of a word like *station*, which gives you the *sh.*

Put them all together and you have:

GH = F

O = I

TI = SH

SO, GHOTI = FISH

If you want to have some fun with your family tonight, do this: when the designated cook asks you what you would like for dinner, tell them that you have a hankering for "goatee and chips"

and then prove to them on paper that you don't actually want a goat, but fish.

HOW TO BUILD A CANDLE

Despite my three university degrees and several awards for writing, I've come to the conclusion that I'm not very smart. This is not false modesty either but a simple statement of fact, which is further supported by the fact that I made a couple of grammatical errors in the paragraph about grammatical errors.

Let me explain. I'm writing this chapter in my study at home. My desk, which is quite sparse because I loathe clutter, contains my laptop, phone, coffee cup, and an aromatic candle that my wonderful wife kindly brought in and lit for me. If any of those items was to break or break down I can either arrange to have it repaired or replaced.

What I can't do is fix them or make another myself from scratch.

Like most people I can't actually do anything. Instead I've learned from the geniuses who have gone before me. Those who have invented incredible things, and then written down how they did it.

Let's unpack this a little further. Of those items listed earlier – laptop, coffee cup, phone, and candle – my best shot at building one from scratch would be the candle. And I'm not inventing it but recreating it.

A candle isn't complicated. Let's face it, we're talking about something that made its first appearance around 500 BCE, so it's hardly modern or complex technology. Excluding the flame, which is an exothermic chemical process (and I only know that because someone wrote it down) my candle has three components.

The wick, the wax, and the glass container.

First, the wick. Looking at it closely now, it appears to be made of three pieces of string that have been braided together, kind of like the way my wife has her hair at the moment. While I know how to braid, from having a whole bunch of daughters, I don't know how to make string. I suppose, as an alternative, I could go out and look for a thin-ish stick to act as a sort of wick substitute.

Okay. We're off to a good start. We have, err – a stick.

Next comes the wax. Now I know from previous readings that the wax used in early candles was made from animal fat. Due to the recent death of our beloved Aslan, a beautiful and beastly Bengal cat, we are now left with little Misty, another Bengal. Unlike Aslan, Misty is tiny and clearly not carrying around much excess fat. Even had she been on the obese side, I wouldn't have the first idea of how to go about extracting the fat from her while keeping her in the land of the living. So having ruled out extracting animal fat from Misty, the best I could hope for would be to collect the earwax from family members, visitors, and delivery people until I had gathered enough to support my stick.

That's two of the three items replicated as best I can. We have a stick and a bunch of earwax.

Finally, the glass container. Having visited one of the famous glassblowing outlets in Venice, Italy, I recall that glass is made by taking a bunch of sand and making it really hot. There was also something about adding in a substance that was, from recollection, called potash. *[Author's note: I know I could look all this up, but in order to maintain the integrity of the experiment, I'm not going to do that.]* So to make the glass container, I would need to schlep out to the beach for some sand, cook it on, say, the BBQ or stove, and toss in a little potash. As I have no idea of what potash is or how to go about getting any, it's clear that I also have zero chance of replicating the glass container.

The only alternative I can think of would be to go out into the garden, dig up some mud, bring it back upstairs to my desk and press it into a sort of round shape.

So there we have it. My attempts to make a candle and its glass container (and we're talking about something that was around for over a thousand years before the start of the Dark Ages) consists of a collection of earwax with a stick wedged in it, which in turn is wrapped in mud. And this is not a new invention but rather something that I'm trying to replicate and is as simple a bit of technology as there is. Because the steps involved in how to make a candle have been written down, however, I'm positive that I could do it by following the instructions.

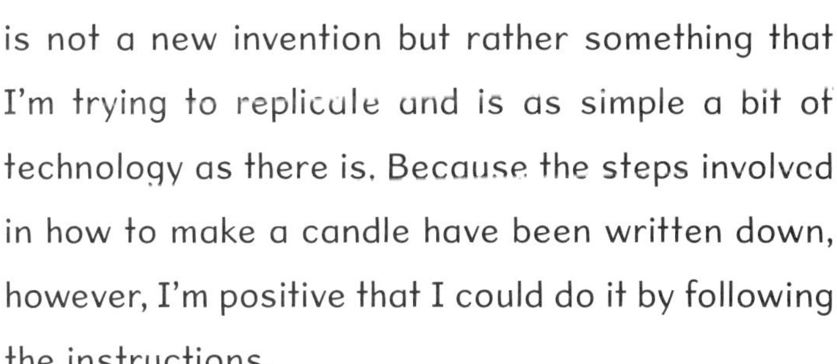

As evidenced by my inability to make a candle, the only thing I can really do is write – and I invented neither the English language nor the alphabet, those 26 squiggles we use to represent the English language on the page.

Despite the interesting and chatty nature of this section, the point of this chapter is supposed to be to help you pass your creative writing test. I've written over 30 books, even so I don't feel particularly confident in this endeavor – the candle idea has got to me. Even if I had not had my candle moment, I would still be reluctant to call myself an expert on writing. But if you do something often enough, if you stick at it, well you're bound to become quite proficient at it, whether it's making a candle, a raft out of sticks, or writing.

WRITE ON

On this occasion, however, rather than rely on the skills and techniques that I have learned and honed over the last 40 years, I am going to turn to the experts in creative writing. And surely there can be no greater experts in a field than those who teach teachers. So in order to show you how to pass your creative writing test, I am going to write a story using my own variation on the Seven Steps to Writing Success which has become so popular in certain schools.

ONE: PLAN

In my experience, the outline of a story can be jotted down on a sticky note. I wrote the outline/plan for my novel, *The Shadow Girl*, on half a sticky note. It reads: "A homeless girl lives on the trains." That's it. The story came alive as I wrote it and my protagonist simply took over and told the story herself. Other characters turned up and did things I didn't expect. In essence, the story took on a life of its own and was as real to me as reality itself. I just wrote down what the characters did. That seven-word outline/plan came in at 120,000 words and over 400 pages. So I'll adopt the same model for the story I'm about to write: `A girl finds a zombie under her little brother's bed.`

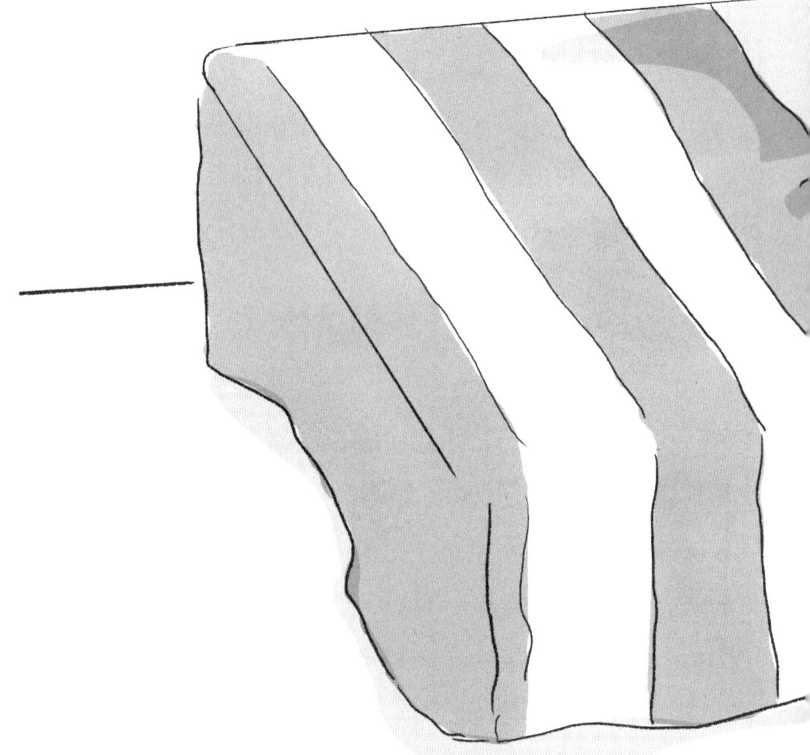

TWO: ENGAGING OPENING

I've gone for this wording because that idea of opening with a "sizzle" has become ubiquitous. It is also an onomatopoeic word, and as teachers seem to love onomatopoeia (despite it being possibly the weakest writing device on the planet) let's start with that. (I think the reason they like it is that ages ago they finally learned how to spell onomatopoeia and then couldn't stop showing off).

Bang, boom, crash went the storm, as outside a car went ZOOOOMING down the road.

Teachers also go on about orientation, which is essentially where the story is set, so we'd better add that in.

Bang, boom, crash went the storm above my house at 15 Darley Street, as outside a car went ZOOOOMING down the road.

THREE: RATCHETING IT UP

Let's see. My opening contains onomatopoeia but it kind of lacks tension, so clearly I have to crank things up bit and maybe throw in some alliteration for good measure. A lot of teachers are mad for alliteration, so I'm going to put plenty in mine.

I glanced under my brother's big, boring, brass, barnacle-shaped bed and discovered, to my immense surprize, a headless zombie with a chainsaw.

FOUR: TALKING NOT CHATTING

This one is fairly obvious. It means that your characters can't just talk about normal, everyday stuff, but rather their talking/dialogue has to be impactful.

"Do you know you have a zombie with a chainsaw under your big, boring, brass, barnacle-shaped bed?" I said to my brother.

Wait a minute. Some teachers believe "said is dead", so we'd better replace it.

"Do you know you have a zombie with a chainsaw under your big, boring, brass, barnacle-shaped bed?" I murmured to my brother.

"Do not!" argued my brother.

"Do too," I opined once more.

FIVE: SHOW, DON'T TELL

This one has been around since the Earth was flat. It's all about painting the picture in the reader's mind without explicitly stating it. So if you come across a character who is unattractive, you don't write Bob was ugly, because that's telling. Instead go for something like Bob possessed the sort of face that only a mother could love. And even then, the mother would have to be a visually impaired orang-utan.

So let's include some "Show, Don't Tell" in the story.

I crawled out of my cool, comfortable, cotton sheets as my auburn locks cascaded down to my sinewy shoulders.

Meanwhile my brother, perhaps wondering if there was indeed a headless zombie with a chainsaw hiding under his big, boring, brass, barnacle-shaped bed, oozed tears of salty sadness.

SIX: KEEP IT INTERESTING

When it comes to keeping it interesting I have to accept that my story is packed full of non-boring stuff. Let's face it, we have a headless zombie with a chainsaw hiding under a bed on a stormy night. There's nothing boring about that.

SEVEN: FINISH WITH A BANG

Clearly this is where I've been going wrong. In all the books I've written, I've tended to go for gentle endings, so that things are kind of okay at the end of the story. It's not happily ever after, but it's not the traditional ending either, I woke up and it was all a dream.

Nor is it the other, more violent, traditional ending, The bus went over a cliff and blew up and we all died. Finishing with a bang is obviously more toward the bus and cliff ending.

Having worked out our ending with a bang, it's now time to stitch our entire story together:

A Zombie Story

by John Larkin

Bang, boom, crash went the storm above my house at 15 Darley Street, as outside a car went ZOOOOMING down the road.

I glanced under my brother's big, boring, brass, barnacle-shaped bed and discovered, to my immense surprize, a headless zombie with a chainsaw.

"Do you know you have a headless zombie with a chainsaw under your big, boring, brass, barnacle-shaped bed?" I murmured to my brother.

"Do not!" argued my brother.

"Do too," I opined once more.

I crawled out of my cool, comfortable, cotton sheets to investigate further as my auburn locks cascaded down to my sinewy shoulders.
Meanwhile my brother, perhaps wondering if there was indeed a headless zombie with a chainsaw hiding under his big, boring, brass, barnacle-shaped bed, oozed tears of salty sadness.

Suddenly, and for no adequately explainable reason, the zombie exploded, showering us both in blood, guts and bits of chainsaw.

THE END

CHAPTER 5
HOW TO AVOID BEING ABDUCTED BY ALIENS

"The official number of humans abducted by aliens currently stands at zero."

The Big Book of Interesting Facts – Volume 16

One of the best places to hide if aliens are coming after you is under your bed. If there's too much stuff wedged under there (such as games, clothes, the family cat, boogie boards, shoeboxes, or the sandwich you didn't eat for school lunch last year that is now generating its own ecosystem) you could try hiding under your sister's bed instead. If your sister is already hiding under there herself, you could chivalrously shove her out so any aliens lurking about will abduct her rather than you.

Wardrobes are another good option. As are pantries, treehouses, the family shed (providing

your family has a shed), the neighbor's shed (providing *they* have a shed), or even up in the ceiling, supposing you can climb up the wall and into that person-hole cover thingy without a ladder. You could also try hiding in a bush or behind a door. Aliens probably won't bother looking for you behind a door, because they don't know what doors are for. To the best of our knowledge there are no doors in outer space, so it's reasonably safe to assume that aliens wouldn't know what to do with a door or think to look for you behind one.

Now you might think that some of the hiding places I've suggested, particularly the behind-the-door one, might seem a bit daft when you are trying to hide from aliens. And you're right. The thing is, however, I can guarantee your safety from aliens in any or all of these hidey-holes for a very simple reason: you have zero chance of being abducted by them. None. Please note: I'm not saying there aren't any aliens. In all honesty I think there are aliens out there. It's just that they are *not* here, nor are they ever likely to be. The distance between our home and theirs (wherever it is) is just too vast.

FAR, FAR AWAY

The nearest star to Earth, after the Sun, is Proxima Centauri, which is approximately 4.2 light-years away. Travelling at the speed of light, which we can't, it would take us a little over four years to reach this system. Travelling in a conventional spacecraft, such as the *Parker Solar Probe*, it would take around 6300 years. And that's our closest neighbor. In galactic terms, (excluding dwarf

and satellite galaxies) our nearest neighbor is Andromeda, which is around 2.5 million light-years away. How long would that trip take in the Parker Solar Probe spacecraft, which can zip along at a fairly nifty 394,800 miles per hour? Let's give it a little perspective. You might think it's a long journey up the coast to visit your grandmother, particularly if you're stuck in the back seat with your annoying siblings. If, on the other hand, you want to pop over to visit the Andromeda Galaxy, the trip would take over 5 billion years, which is a seriously long time, especially if you're still in the back seat with your siblings. And then of course, you have to make the journey home. Even if you leave early in order to beat the traffic, it's still going to be a 10 billion-year round trip. So make sure you visit the bathroom before heading off.

IS THERE **ANYBODY** OUT THERE?

As you can see, the distances between us and, well, anywhere else in the cosmos are literally astronomical. According to Albert Einstein we are bound by the universal speed limit, which is the speed of light – 186,000 miles per second. The speed of light is pretty quick, but in universal terms it is rather pedestrian. And light can only travel at light speed because it has zero mass. Anything that has mass – you, me, spacecraft, Santa Claus – cannot travel at light speed, as to do so would require an infinite amount of energy. And nothing can go faster than the speed of light.

THE DRAKE EQUATION

In 1961 the astrophysicist Frank Drake (1930–2022) thought it would be interesting to try and calculate the probability of intelligent life existing elsewhere in the Milky Way. In order to facilitate this he created an equation – the Drake Equation – which is still used today. Even using conservative estimates for the seven factors of the equation, the number of planets in the Milky Way that could contain intelligent life is staggeringly high.

Before delving any further into the Drake Equation, we might want to first consider what constitutes "intelligent" life. As astounding as it seems, we may yet find life in our own solar system. For instance, it is thought one of Jupiter's moons, Europa, could support life because there is evidence of liquid water beneath its icy crust. Liquid water is an essential component for life to emerge. Because of Europa's distance from the habitable/ Goldilocks zone, however, even if life is discovered there, such life won't be anything like you and me. It's more than likely to be microbes, which are not exactly a whole lot of fun to be around. If you doubt this, try inviting a bunch of microbes to your next birthday party. Chances are, rather than run around with nerf guns and involve themselves in other party games and join in the "Happy Birthday" song, they'll just squiggle around in a Petri dish in their party hats. And due to microbes' non-existent disposable income, it is highly unlikely they will bring you a present either.

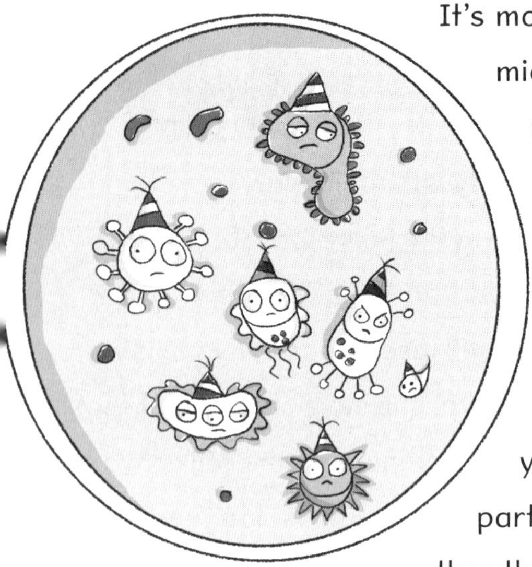

In our search for extraterrestrial life (that is life beyond our own planet) we need to be looking for species that are capable of conceiving, designing and then engineering advanced technology. In other words – beings not too dissimilar from us. That we, on occasion, use that technology to blow each other to smithereens over some squabble or other, would probably mean that we belong in the "spectacularly daft" category as well. But as our own species continues to showcase, it is possible to be both.

Dolphins, ravens, and certain breeds of dogs, for example, might be considered intelligent; but none of them, at the time of writing, have invented even the crudest form of technology, let alone a device capable of sending communiqués out into the cosmos. And while it might seem unfair to define intelligence purely on human terms (dolphins, for example, might think we're incredibly daft for heating up the planet to a hazardous point), for the sake of this exercise that is the criteria that we will work with. We are, in essence, looking for technologically advanced aliens who, like ourselves, will be using their advanced technology to look for us.

So what is the Drake Equation? And just how many planets are estimated to be out there in the Milky Way that could contain intelligent life?

The Drake Equation looks like this:

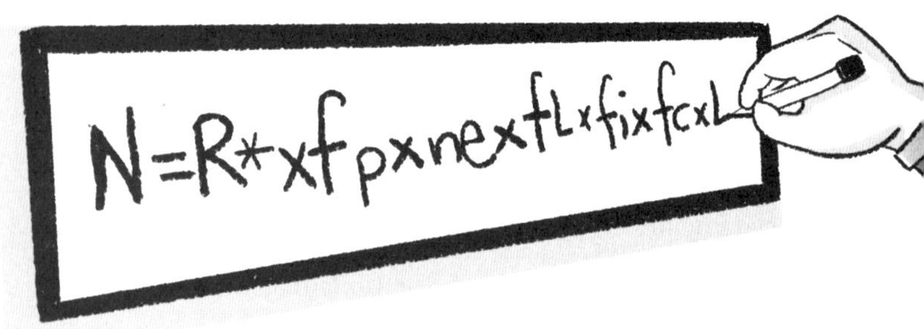

Although this might look like something you might see on Sheldon's whiteboard in an episode of *The Big Bang Theory*, it is actually not that complicated and can be easily understood and explained by a non-scientist such as me. So let's start by breaking down the factors that make up the Drake Equation.

N is the total of all the other factors. In other words, N is the answer we are looking for. And what we are looking for is the number of technologically advanced civilisations in our galaxy that are actively broadcasting their presence.

The seven factors that we use to calculate **N** are as follows:

R* is the average rate of star formation in our galaxy suitable for the development of life.

fp is the number of stars that have planetary systems such as our own star, the Sun.

ne is the number of planets, per solar system, with an environment suitable for life.

fL is the number of habitable planets where life emerges.

fi is the number of these life-bearing planets where intelligent life actually evolves.

fc is the number of intelligent civilizations that develop technology to the point where it can communicate, or attempt to communicate, with other extraterrestrial civilisations.

L is the length of time that those civilisations have existed.

Unfortunately the Drake Equation cannot be solved because we only know the value of the first factor (**R*** – the average rate of star formation in our galaxy) and have to estimate the values of the other six factors. Frank Drake himself put the figure somewhere between 1,000 and 100,000,000. That's up to one hundred million Earth-like planets in our galaxy that have aliens capable of communicating with us. Let's state that again: ONE HUNDRED MILLION planets that ET could conceivably phone and call home.

It is interesting to note that we didn't join the **fc** community until very recently. Although radio waves have been transmitted since 1899 it wasn't until 1974 that the first radio waves were deliberately sent out into the cosmos, specifically directed at the M13 star cluster. Radio waves, like light, contain no mass and so move at the speed of light. Still, the radio waves directed toward M13 won't reach it for 25,000 years and by the time they do, the star cluster probably won't be in the same spot so the message will miss it anyway.

The Drake Equation, it should be noted, was never meant to provide an accurate answer to the question that it proposes, but rather its purpose is to engender and foster discussion, debate, and further research on the topic.

WoW!

Although we are transmitting radio waves to the cosmos, you might be wondering if we are actively listening for the same from distant alien civilisations. Well the answer is yes. SETI (Search for Extraterrestrial Intelligence), for example, is doing just that. SETI has had its ears (satellite dishes) turned to the heavens since 1984. You might also be wondering if we have ever found anything. Again, and this might come as a bit of a shock, the answer is yes. In 1977 a radio burst emanating from the Sagittarius star system (not star sign) and lasting 72 seconds was discovered by astronomer Jerry R. Ehman through the Big Ear radio telescope, which was part of the Ohio State University's program. The signal was over 30 times louder than the baseline. This possible first contact has become ubiquitously known as the “Wow! signal”, and was named after the onomatopoeic palindrome that Ehman wrote in the margin of the computer printout of the signal. Unfortunately,

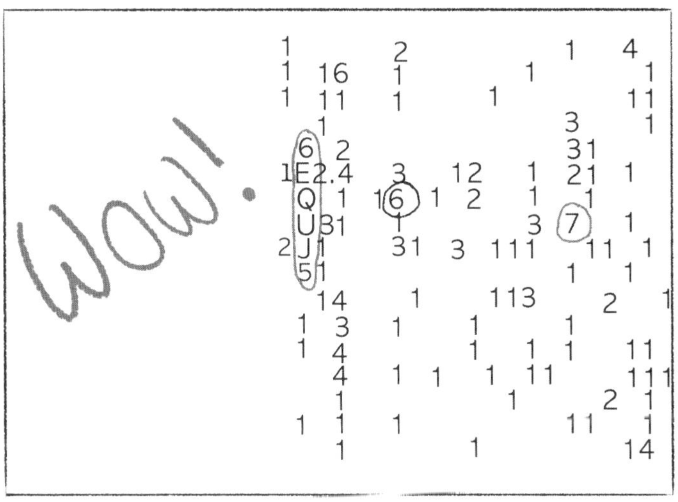

despite repeated efforts that continue to this day, the Wow! signal is all we have heard from the stars that might have an alien origin. Since that day the cosmos has lapsed back into a protracted and eerie silence.

THE FERMI PARADOX

The Fermi paradox takes the Drake Equation and essentially says, "Okay. Given the millions of Earth-like planets out there, where is everyone? Why hasn't ET phoned us yet?" Although the Fermi paradox appears to take its lead from the Drake Equation, the Fermi paradox actually came first. One lunchtime in 1950 the Italian physicist Enrico Fermi (1901–1954) posed the question, "Where is everyone?" Please note, he wasn't asking why so few of their colleagues had joined them for lunch, but rather, given the mathematical certainty of intelligent life emerging elsewhere in our galaxy, he was wondering why it hadn't made contact yet. It is, nonetheless, an intriguing question, but because it requires more speculation than it does mathematical computations, it is more a philosophical question.

If there are countless Earth-like planets out there in the Milky Way, let's look at some of the reasons that may be behind the lack of contact.

OUT OF TIME

Apart from the staggering distances involved, as discussed earlier in this chapter, there are a number of other reasons as to why no one has contacted us yet.

Despite the mathematical improbability as per the Drake Equation, it might turn out to be just us after all. Life could be rarer in the universe than we think. Despite the diversity of life on our planet, it could be that Earth is the ultimate outlier and there is no other life elsewhere in the entire universe, let alone our galaxy. Although you could argue that without life forms to admire it, the universe is kind of pointless.

Or it could be there once was life out there, it's just that over time it may well have gone extinct. Who even knows how long we'll have at the top of the Earth's food chain before we manage to wipe ourselves out by destroying the planet. However, given our penchant for self-destruction, it might turn out not to be very long at all.

THE DARK FOREST

Another couple of potential reasons that ET hasn't visited us yet could be because we're too violent or too dull to bother with. Any alien species capable of circumventing the laws of physics and making their way here, would need to be mind-numbingly intelligent. They might then consider us the intellectual equivalent of termites by comparison. There is a school of thought that says aliens could already be present on Earth but in a form that we don't or cannot recognize.

The Dark Forest theory postulates that the universe is a dark forest where you are either hunter or hunted. Given what we are capable of, other intelligent life forms might choose to hide from us for fear of extermination.

If you chuckle at the thought of humans being the exterminators of the universe, you might want to consider the number of species we have managed to exterminate on our own planet. The sweet-natured flightless dodo bird was doing rather well for itself before it encountered humans. Once we arrived on the scene, the dodo lasted a further 100 years before the last of its number supposedly met its end on a beach at the hands of a sailor, who presumably thought clubbing a harmless bird to death would be a bit of a hoot.

As a species we are capable of so much goodness, but we are also exceedingly violent. We are, by far and away, the most brutal species ever to roam this planet or possibly any other. Less than a century ago, a short Austrian psychopath with a silly moustache attempted to annihilate an entire race of people on the basis that he happened to not like them very much. Adolf Hitler and his Nazi minions killed approximately 6 million Jewish people during the Holocaust. Overall, between the fighting, bombing and subsequent disease epidemics, between 70 and 85 million people were killed during the Second World War.

Even genius scientists can get caught up in the violence, at least indirectly. Our dear friend Enrico Fermi, while employed on the Manhattan Project, was heavily involved in development of the world's first nuclear weapon, which would kill approximately 200,000 when dropped on the cities of Hiroshima and Nagasaki. And that was just the initial blast and doesn't count those who would later die of radiation poisoning.

MARS
HOT
SPOTS

Given the above, if you were an alien, would you be in a rush to make contact with us? I for one would give planet Earth a very wide berth. And if Aliens want to colonize Earth, we are so brilliant at killing ourselves, there really is no need for aliens to get involved. They may as well just wait for us to do it for them. Although unlikely, it is not even beyond the realms of comprehension that the current superpowers' presidents could blow up the world out of spite.

Despite the opening to this chapter where I suggested the best hiding spots to scurry to should aliens turn up, in all seriousness if there is any hiding to be done, it will be the aliens hiding behind doors from us. Or maybe, like the aliens, and for the sake of our survival as a species, we may yet evolve out of our violent ways. But that will come down to future generations.

IT WILL COME DOWN TO YOU.

BEFORE YOU GO...
A FINAL WORD(S)!

What do you call a bunch of words that don't mean what they mean? An idiom. That's right, with an M. Or sometimes it might just be plain slang, but either way, it's a good way to get your point across, or to sound silly. Either one!

FLAT OUT LIKE A LIZARD DRINKING
Busy

ONYA BIKE
An invitation to leave

PUT A SOCK IN IT
An invitation to be quiet

COULDN'T PUNCH YOUR WAY OUT OF A WET PAPER BAG
To be incompetent

WRAP YOUR LAUGHING GEAR 'ROUND THAT
An invitation to eat

FAIR SUCK OF THE SAUCE BOTTLE
A plea for equal treatment

BEAT AROUND THE BUSH
Avoiding the subject

SPILL THE BEANS
Telling a secret

ROUGH END OF THE PINEAPPLE
A raw deal

DOG'S BREAKFAST
A mess

UNDER THE WEATHER
Feeling unwell

FAIR DINKUM
True

IT'S IN THE BAG
Guaranteed success

PULL THE WOOL OVER YOUR EYES
Tricking someone

ABOUT THE AUTHOR

John Larkin is a multi-award-winning author. His 2012 novel, *The Shadow Girl*, won the Victorian Premier's Literary Award while *The Pause* won the 2015 Queensland Literary Award and was shortlisted for the CBCA Book of the Year Award for Older Readers. He is the writer-in-residence at Knox Grammar School, University of Technology Sydney, and All Saints Anglican School (Gold Coast).

ABOUT THE ILLUSTRATOR

Chrissie Krebs is the author-illustrator of several picture books, including *Pig in a Wig* and *There is Something Weird in Santa's Beard.* She has also illustrated picture books such as *A Dinosaur Ate Dad's Hair* and the 2018 CBCA Children's Book of the Year for Early Childhood, *Rodney Loses It!* and its sequel, *Rodney Forgets It!* (2022) She is the author and illustrator of the graphic novel series, *Mack and Cheeze*, and also *Bizard the Bear Wizard* (2023). Chrissie is living her inner four-year-old's dream, and cannot believe she gets paid to draw pictures all day.